WHERE BiRDS AND MONKEYS PLAY

RAiN FOREST ANiMALS

By MARK OBLINGER

Illustrated by RYAN WHEATCROFT

CANTATA
LEARNING
MANKATO, MINNESOTA

WWW.CANTATALEARNING.COM

CANTATA
LEARNING
MANKATO, MINNESOTA

Published by Cantata Learning
1710 Roe Crest Drive
North Mankato, MN 56003
www.cantatalearning.com

Library of Congress Control Number: 2014956989
978-1-63290-255-9 (hardcover/CD)
978-1-63290-407-2 (paperback/CD)
978-1-63290-449-2 (paperback)

Where Birds and Monkeys Play: Rain Forest Animals by Mark Oblinger
Illustrated by Ryan Wheatcroft

Book design, Tim Palin Creative
Editorial direction, Flat Sole Studio
Executive musical production and direction, Elizabeth Draper
Music arranged and produced by Mark Oblinger

Printed in the United States of America.

A Donation has been made to the
Clay County Public Library In
Memory Of:

Lillian White

This Donation has been made by:

Dennis & Jane Miller
Sara & Moses Martinez
Nathan & Jaclyn Miller

VISIT
WWW.CANTATALEARNING.COM/ACCESS-OUR-MUSIC
TO SING ALONG TO THE SONG

Rain forest trees stay green all year. These forests are usually in areas that get a lot of rain and where the weather is hot. Rain forests are found around the world but only cover a small part of Earth. But they are home to more than half of all animal, plant, and insect **species**!

Now turn the page, and sing along.

Rain forest, rain forest,
where the birds and the monkeys play.

Half the species in the world
live in them today.

Rain forest, rain forest,
always wet and green.

Half the species in the world,
and some we've never seen!

Birds and bats and great big cats,
there are **creatures** high and low.

Slithering snakes, frogs on logs,
and sloths that move real slow.

Some butterflies' wings look like eyes.

Some bugs look like sticks.

To keep away the things that prey,
camouflage is a sneaky trick!

Rain forest, rain forest,
where the birds and the monkeys play.

Half the species in the world
live in them today.

Rain forest, rain forest,
always wet and green.

Half the species in the world,
and some we've never seen!

Frogs and salamanders hunt
for bugs or squishy slugs to eat.

Crocodiles and giant snakes
prey on animals they meet!

In the branches, keeping cool
above the jungle floor,
sleeps the spotted jaguar.

It's time to **pounce** and roar!

17

And don't forget the toucans!
Each one has a giant beak
as colorful as a rainbow.
Some even have blue feet!

Rain forest, rain forest,
where the birds and
the monkeys play.

Half the species in the world
live in them today.

Rain forest, rain forest,
always wet and green.

Half the species in the world
and some we've never seen!

SONG LYRICS
Where Birds and Monkeys Play: Rain Forest Animals

Rain forest, rain forest,
where the birds and the monkeys play.

Half the species in the world
live in them today.

Rain forest, rain forest,
always wet and green.

Half the species in the world,
and some we've never seen!

Birds and bats and great big cats,
there are creatures high and low.

Slithering snakes, frogs on logs,
and sloths that move real slow.

Some butterflies' wings look like eyes.
Some bugs look like sticks.

To keep away the things that prey,
camouflage is a sneaky trick!

Rain forest, rain forest,
where the birds and the monkeys play.

Half the species in the world
live in them today.

Rain forest, rain forest,
always wet and green.

Half the species in the world,
and some we've never seen!

Frogs and salamanders hunt
for bugs or squishy slugs to eat.

Crocodiles and giant snakes
prey on animals they meet!

In the branches, keeping cool
above the jungle floor,
sleeps the spotted jaguar.

It's time to pounce and roar!

And don't forget the toucans!
Each one has a giant beak
as colorful as a rainbow.
Some even have blue feet!

Rain forest, rain forest,
where the birds and the monkeys play.

Half the species in the world
live in them today.

Rain forest, rain forest,
always wet and green.

Half the species in the world
and some we've never seen!

Where Birds and Monkeys Play: Rain Forest Animals

Chorus

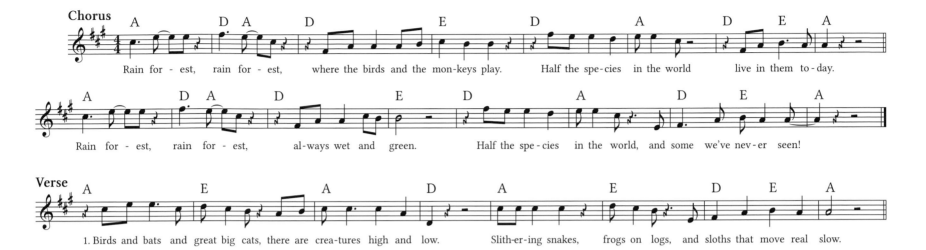

Rain for - est, rain for - est, where the birds and the mon-keys play. Half the spe-cies in the world live in them to - day.

Rain for - est, rain for - est, al-ways wet and green. Half the spe-cies in the world, and some we've nev-er seen!

Verse

1. Birds and bats and great big cats, there are crea-tures high and low. Slith-er-ing snakes, frogs on logs, and sloths that move real slow.

Verse 2
Some butterflies' wings look like eyes.
Some bugs look like sticks
To keep away the things that prey,
camouflage is a sneaky trick!

Verse 3
Frogs and salamanders hunt
for bugs or squishy slugs to eat.
Crocodiles and giant snakes
prey on the animals they meet!

Verse 4
In the branches, keeping cool
above the jungle floor,
sleeps the spotted jaguar.
It's time to pounce and roar!

Chorus

Bridge

And don't for - get the tou - cans! Each one has a gi - ant beak as col - or - ful as a

rain - bow. Some e - ven have blue feet!

Chorus

GLOSSARY

creatures—living beings

camouflage—coloring that helps animals hide in their natural surroundings

pounce—to quickly jump on something and grab it

prey—to hunt, catch, and eat another animal

slithering—sliding along like a snake

species—animals, plants, or insects that are alike in certain ways

GUIDED READING ACTIVITIES

1. Why do you think the author picked the title *Where Birds and Monkeys Play* for this book?

2. What other animals can you think of that live in rain forests?

3. Who is the illustrator of this book? What is your favorite illustration, and why?

TO LEARN MORE

Allgor, Marie. *Endangered Rain Forest Animals*. New York: PowerKids Press, 2013.

Levete, Sarah. *Life in the Rain Forest*. Mankato, MN: Capstone, 2010.

Matthews, Rupert. *Rain Forest Explorer*. New York: DK Publishing, 2014.

Scott, Janine. *Rain Forest Life*. Mankato, MN: Capstone, 2012.